Divided We Stand

The American Conquest Strategy

by
Jwanna Savoie-Powell

Divided We Stand

The American Conquest Strategy

Table of Contents

Introduction

The chronicles of nations are often marked by their capacity for conquest, both within and beyond their borders. The narrative of the United States, a relatively young player on the historical stage, is no exception. Its ascent to prominence has been paved with strategies, tactics, and policies aimed at expansion and control. These strategies, while initially focused on territorial growth, have evolved into subtler forms of dominance - the conquest of minds, markets, and political influence.

The American conquest strategy is a subject that weighs heavily on the trajectory of our society. Its tendrils extend into the soil of our shared history, wrapping around the roots of our cultural fabric, and influence the very way we perceive ourselves and others. This book aims to dissect these complex strategies, laying them bare for us all to examine.

Understanding these strategies is not merely an academic exercise, but a crucial imperative for deciphering the broader consequences that befall our daily lives. Whether we're conscious of it or not, the American approach to expansion has shaped our perceptions, our environment, and the very essence of how our society functions.

Consider the political landscape, riven with divisions that often seem insurmountable. Or reflect upon the economic chasms that yawn wider with each passing year, fostering discontent and strife. Each of these modern challenges can be traced, at least in part, to strategies conceived with an eye towards dominance and often at the expense of unity and equality.

The nuanced understanding of these conquest strategies provides a prism through which we can view not only past actions but also contemporary events. It can guide our interpretations of the policies that govern us, the media narratives that inform us, and the social dynamics that often divide us. But more importantly, it lends us a perspective to consider the path ahead—an insight into how we might cultivate a more equitable and united future.

As we embark on this exploration, it's important to acknowledge the complexity and the multifaceted nature of this topic. The strategies employed throughout American history have been deeply intertwined with global events and shaped by myriad internal and external pressures. They are not the product of any single individual, party, or ideology but rather a web of converging interests and opportunistic maneuvers.

The approach to this exposition will be one of careful examination and balanced critique. We aim to inform, certainly, but also to encourage critical thought and reflection on the part of the reader. Each revelation about the past is presented not as a condemnation but as a stepping stone to greater awareness, inviting readers to draw their conclusions and engage with the material in a meaningful way.

Our exploration begins at the roots, with the very strategies that laid the groundwork for future divisions—an assessment of how historical precursors and colonial strategies set a precedent for contemporary American tactics. From there, we will branch out to examine how ideological wedges have been driven into the heart of society, often aided by media and propaganda engineered to craft and control public opinion.

In the ensuing chapters, we will navigate the turbulent waters of political ruptures, dissecting the mechanics of elections, the deliberate manipulation of districting, and the consequent impact on our governance. Similarly, we will confront the economic divides that have become a defining aspect of American life, evaluating the wealth gap and the effect of policies on societal polarization.

Our journey will take us through the maze of social fragmentation, where race, ethnicity, and the ongoing immigration debates provide critical case studies in division. The narrative will expand to a global stage, where American tactics abroad have both influenced and reflected domestic endeavors—how the echo of American strategy reverberates across continents, affecting foreign divisions.

Yet, while the book scrutinizes the deep-seated fissures that challenge us, it also serves to uncover paths to reconciliation. In the final chapter, we will explore the avenues for overcoming these divisions, seeking out the possible futures of unity that may yet lie ahead for us all.

Let's embark on this journey with an open mind and an understanding that the strategies of conquest are not relics of a distant past but active elements shaping our present and future. The goal is not just to inform but to transform our collective awareness, empowering us to recognize and perhaps even dismantle the architectural framework of division that constrains us.

The reality is that the American conquest strategy affects everyone—our families, our communities, our nation, and our world. Gaining an in-depth perspective on these tactics is about more than understanding the past; it's about reclaiming the present and reimagining the future. The knowledge gained through these pages is a tool, one that has the potential to reshape the landscape of American life, if wielded with wisdom and precision.

The task before us is as challenging as it is enlightening. It requires us to face uncomfortable truths, reevaluate long-held beliefs, and piece together a mosaic of realities that reside in the gray areas of our history and psyche. It's time to peel back the layers of strategic conquest that have, for better or worse, defined the American condition.

And so, with a sense of both urgency and importance, we turn the page to delve into the intricate tapestry of the American conquest strategy—understanding its foundation, its ramifications, and the hope that knowledge might pave the way for a more united, just, and peaceful society.

Chapter 1:
The Roots of Division

The formative years of America's historical narrative present a complex tapestry of ambition interwoven with strategic exploitation. At the heart of this burgeoning nation's trek towards sovereignty and power lay a series of calculated colonial strategies, sowing the initial seeds of discord that would later flourish into broad societal rifts. As we explore the origins of these divisions, it's essential to consider the prevailing attitudes and methods employed by colonial powers that prioritized territorial acquisition and economic gain over indigenous rights and equanimity. These actions were not without consequence, imprinting a legacy of fragmentation on the land and its people—a legacy that has proven both indelible and influential. This chapter aims to dissect the early methodologies and mindsets that established a pattern of division, setting the stage for a systemic schism that has become deeply embedded in the American conscience and modus operandi.

Historical Precursors

The division slicing through the fabric of American society didn't emerge in a vacuum. It's rooted deeply in a past where imperial ambitions set the stage for a culture predicated on conquest and control. Historical precursors to today's fissures can be traced back to the colonization strategies employed by European powers in the New World. These early approaches prioritized territorial expansion and resource extraction, often at the expense of indigenous populations and without regard for subsequent societal impacts. This legacy of exploitation laid down the patterns of dominance and subordination that persist in modern power structures, seeping into the consciousness of a burgeoning nation. It's essential to recognize these origins to fully grasp the entrenched nature of the divisions we now confront. As the strategies of the colonial era established an enduring framework, they set in motion a tradition of division that would be reinvented through the centuries, compelling us toward a reckoning with the very foundations upon which the nation was built.

The Colonial Strategies In understanding the roots of division in America, we must delve into the colonial strategies implemented during the nation's infancy. The earliest European settlers brought with them notions of dominance and exploitation which they established as part of the fundamental framework within the New World. They developed specific strategies to maintain control over the vast territories and diverse populations they encountered, the repercussions of which echo into the modern socio-political landscape.

One such strategy was the establishment of the encomienda system, which was a form of forced labor imposed upon indigenous populations. It allowed the settlers to claim labor and allegiance from native communities, stripping them of their autonomy. While the system was mainly employed by the Spanish, its essence was mirrored in the practices of other colonial powers. By creating a tiered society with the colonialists at the top, the seeds of a class system were sown.

Another tactical measure used by colonizers was the deliberate fracturing of indigenous tribes. By promoting rivalries and exacerbating pre-existing conflicts between different groups, colonial powers maintained a weakened and divided native opposition. This divide and rule approach prevented cohesive resistance and allowed for easier management and control of the territory.

A key component of colonial strategies involved the manipulation of land ownership. Land grants and the promise of property enticed many Europeans to venture to the New World. However, this often led to the displacement of native populations and the concentration of wealth and power in the hands of a few. The establishment of plantations and large estates would go on to influence socio-economic relations for centuries.

Religious strategies also played a significant role. The spread of Christianity was both a mission and a method of control, with conversion often presented as a condition for receiving basic rights and amenities. This not only suppressed indigenous belief systems but also served to morally justify the harsh treatment of non-Christian populations.

Moreover, the introduction and implementation of European laws and governance structures were aimed at solidifying control. The colonists' legal frameworks were imposed with little regard for local customs and laws, establishing a legal system that benefitted the occupiers and facilitated the exploitation of both land and people.

Trade and economic policies were manipulated to ensure the dependency of the colonies on the mother countries. Mercantilism ensured the flow of resources and wealth from America to Europe, while inhibiting the economic development of the colonies. By controlling trade, colonial powers could ensure the profitability of the colonies while preventing the emergence of economic competitors.

In addition to economic control, the physical layouts of colonies were designed to serve colonial interests. Town planning, the construction of forts and roads, and the strategic placement of settlements were all directed at maximizing control over territory and resources, often with military strategy in mind. The infrastructure established during colonial times set the stage for the development of transportation and trade networks that continue to influence American geography.

The mandated use of European languages and educational systems further entrenched colonial dominance, ensuring future generations of colonials and indigenous people alike would adopt the values and norms of the ruling powers. This linguistic and cultural homogenization was yet another way in which colonial strategies ensured sustained control over the populace.

Colonial strategies also included alliances with certain tribes or groups to exert control over others. The playing off of one group against another secured colonial interests and prevented the unification of disparate groups in rebellion against the settlers. This tactic of manipulation and balance-of-power diplomacy was a prevalent theme throughout the colonial era.

It's essential to highlight the role of African slavery within these colonial strategies. The transatlantic slave trade and the systematic dehumanization of African slaves were not only a gross violation of human rights but also a calculated method of building a labor force that would sustain the agricultural economies of the colonies. The legacy of slavery has had lasting effects on racial dynamics in the United States.

The colonies' dependence on European goods and resources essentially created a form of economic colonialism. This dependence stunted local craftsmanship and industry and ensured that the colonies remained tied to the economic interests of their colonial masters. This relationship laid the groundwork for tensions that would later culminate in the struggle for American independence.

Relations with European adversaries also played a role in the colonial calculus. For instance, the French and Indian War from 1754 to 1763 was as much about contesting territory as it was about positioning in global geopolitics. Colonial strategies often leveraged these international rivalries to strengthen their own position in the New World.

Gender roles and family structures were not immune to colonial strategies. By imposing European gender norms and family hierarchies, colonists aimed to disrupt the social cohesion of indigenous and enslaved peoples. This dislocation was intended to subvert existing community bonds and replace them with the patriarchal models prevalent among the colonists.

In conclusion, the mosaic of colonial strategies used during America's founding era established a legacy of division that is woven into the fabric of contemporary society. Understanding this historical context is instrumental in grasping the complex nature of present-day political, economic, and social divides. As we reflect on this heritage, we acknowledge the deep-seated challenges that stem from the nation's inception—a narrative critical for any discourse on American unity and the pursuit of a more equitable future.

Chapter 2:
Ideological Wedges

Understanding the roots of division illuminates the role of ideologies in driving wedges within the societal fabric. The strategic employment of belief systems acts as the fulcrum upon which the lever of American conquest strategy pivots, furthering goals by dividing to conquer. Ideologies are not merely adopted organically but are often forged and implanted through calculated measures, becoming instruments of influence that shape and polarize public discourse. These wedges, exploited by various agencies, disseminate through the channels of communication—undermining consensus and sowing discord. It's crucial, therefore, to dissect how these conceptual chisels are crafted and driven home, forever altering the landscape of collective consciousness, paving the way for dominion. As this chapter will unravel, the implementation of these wedges serves not only as a tool for internal cohesion but also becomes a beacon that guides the nation's approach to international engagement, manifesting a grand strategy with both domestic and global repercussions.

Media and Propaganda

In the discordant symphony of division, media and propaganda function as ceaseless conductors, wielding unprecedented influence on the public psyche. Central to America's conquest strategy, these tools magnify ideological wedges, meticulously curating narratives that echo across the socio-political spectrum. Within this machinery of persuasion, media entities are not neutral messengers but active participants in the crafting of reality, enveloping audiences in a milieu that reinforces division. Propaganda, masquerading as ubiquitous information, insidiously shapes perceptions, manufacturing consent or dissent where expedient. This section dissects the sophisticated orchestration of media and propaganda and how their synergy generates chasms in the societal quarry, pushing the masses into enclaves of echo chambers and partisanship. Understanding their role is imperative in comprehending the full mosaic of America's conquest strategy and its pervasive impact on our collective existence.

Crafting Public Opinion In the nuanced interplay of contemporary society, the construction of public opinion is not merely incidental; it's an intricate art, one that has been fine-tuned to an unprecedented level of sophistication. As we delve into the mechanisms by which public sentiment is shaped, it is essential to contemplate not only the techniques themselves but also their profound implications for the American conquest strategy.

The instrumentality of media in the orchestration of public opinion is of particular significance. Media entities, through their reporting, commentary and, increasingly, social media presence, have the unparalleled capability to set the national agenda. It's through this agenda-setting process that certain issues are highlighted while others are marginalized, thus directing the public's attention and concern to specific areas.

In the realm of this discourse, the pertinence of framing cannot be overstated. By presenting information in a particular light or context, media can subtly influence the interpretation and perception of news events. This, in turn, can modify attitudes and eventually lead to a shift in public consensus on various issues, aligning with strategic objectives outlined by powers at be.

Moreover, the use of political spin and public relations campaigns further refines the image being projected. Political figures and institutions craft messages to resonate with core values and emotions of their target demographics. Through a careful selection of words and imagery, they manage to instill a particular narrative in the collective consciousness of the public.

It is in this sphere where symbolism and the power of repetition come into play. Messages that are repeated often enough, especially ones replete with symbolic significance, tend to be accepted as truth. This phenomenon can be leveraged to elicit support for policies or to redirect the public's focus from potentially contentious issues.

The strategy also involves controlling the flow of information. Access to certain pieces of information can be restricted or released strategically to influence public opinion. Leaks, timed disclosures, and even misinformation serve as tools to shape the narrative in a desired direction.

The emergence of digital media has exponentially increased the avenues through which public opinion can be crafted. Social media platforms, with their algorithms that favor engagement, often prioritize content that is sensational or that reinforces existing beliefs, a practice known as 'echo chamber' formation. Such environments greatly amplify messages that align with the attitudes and opinions of specific groups.

Not to be overlooked is the role of influencers or opinion leaders in disseminating and reinforcing messages. These individuals, with their large followings and perceived authority, can effectively sway public opinion through endorsements or critiques. Their involvement acts as a force multiplier in the spread of certain narratives.

Public opinion is also molded through the selective presentation of polling data and statistics. The way in which this data is interpreted and shared can create perceptions of consensus or division that may not accurately reflect the nuances of public thought.

Emotional appeals and fear tactics are another cornerstone in the craft of public opinion. By playing on fears, real or perceived, a sense of urgency is created, pushing the public toward a desired response. Simultaneously, emotional narratives can foster identification with a cause or group, further solidifying the directed sentiment.

It's essential to recognize the ethical implications inherent in these tactics. While they are powerful tools in steering public opinion, they can also potentially undermine democratic ideals when used irresponsibly. The manipulation of public sentiment can lead to a populace that is less informed, more polarized, and increasingly distrustful of the very institutions meant to represent them.

Despite the existence of regulatory frameworks intended to maintain fairness and transparency in information dissemination, there remain significant challenges in accountability and enforcement. In an era where information is abundant and sources are manifold, maintaining oversight is more complex than ever.

On an individual level, the need for media literacy has become paramount. In order to navigate the torrents of information and strategic messaging, the public must be equipped to critically analyze sources, recognize bias, and understand underlying motives in the presentation of news and information.

As we ponder over the ways in which public opinion is meticulously crafted, it is imperative to maintain awareness of the broader strategy at play. These tactics, while narrowing on the immediacy of current events and policy debates, serve a grander purpose within the overarching approach of American conquest strategy. This strategy encompasses not only domestic but global aspirations, and it is set against a canvas that is as much about power and control as it is about governance and public service.

Understanding the complexity of crafting public opinion is thus pivotal, not only for comprehending current events but also for anticipating the trajectories of influence that shape the world we live in. Fostering an informed and engaged public is not merely beneficial; it is essential for the sustainability of democratic society in the face of potent strategic maneuvers designed to sway the collective will.

Chapter 3:
Political Ruptures

In the woven fabric of American conquest strategy, the thread of political discord is particularly pronounced, and in Chapter 3, "Political Ruptures," we delve into the origins and consequences of these divisions. As we've traversed the historical and ideological landscapes that have carved out the nation's collective psyche, it becomes evident that the very systems designed to facilitate democratic expression are not immune to exploitation. Within the realm of election mechanics, a confluence of factors converges to shape not just the outcomes, but the very arena in which the American political battle is waged. The manipulation of districting, the arcane intricacies of voter registration, and the ever-controversial practice of gerrymandering form the crux of this discourse. These political fissures don't simply reflect divergent viewpoints but are engineered barriers to representation which have distorted the democratic process and amplified polarization to unprecedented levels. This chapter aims to untangle these deliberate constrivances, to reveal not just the profound impact they have on governance but also to scrutinize how they reflect a broader strategy of control that extends far beyond the shores of the United States.

Election Mechanics

The mechanics underpinning the electoral process have, without a doubt, accentuated the fault lines splintering the American political landscape. As we peer closer at the intricate gears of this machinery, we find that its design isn't just a matter of counting ballots—it's a finely tuned system capable of shaping the very nature of political power. The intricate web of laws and regulations governing the casting and counting of votes, the allocation of delegates, and the certification of outcomes serves not merely as the backbone of democracy, but as a stealthy lever for strategic conquest. With the rising importance of data analytics and targeted campaigning, every nuance in the electoral process can be—and is—exploited to swing the delicate pendulum of power. As this section unfolds, we see that it's not merely about who casts the votes, but who counts them, how they're counted, and the hidden hands that may be tipping the scales beneath the veneer of unfettered democracy.

Gerrymandering and Districting is a practice with deep historical roots, intrinsically linked to the political ruptures of contemporary America. As part of a wider conquest strategy, the manipulation of electoral boundaries both reflects and exacerbates partisan divides, posing grave concerns for the democratic process. To grasp the significant impact of this practice, one must understand the dual processes of gerrymandering and districting as fixtures of political influence.

Gerrymandering occurs when political groups modify electoral district boundaries to create an advantage for a particular party or group. By manipulating these lines, they can maximize the number of districts that favor one party and minimize those that favor the opposition. This technique warps districts into convoluted shapes, often resulting in communities being split and their collective voice being diluted.

While districting, the drawing of electoral boundaries, is necessary for the allocation of political representation, it becomes problematic when it transitions from a process driven by neutrality to one driven by partisan or factional gain. The fairness of districting speaks to the core of representative democracy: each vote should carry equal weight, and communities should have a chance to be meaningfully represented.

The origins of gerrymandering in the United States can be traced back to the early 1800s when Governor Elbridge Gerry of Massachusetts approved a district shape that was said to resemble a salamander. But this act was not an isolated incident; rather, it was a formalization of the tactics often used subtly by those in power to maintain their control.

Strategies for district manipulation can be categorized mainly into two techniques: 'packing' and 'cracking.' Packing involves concentrating opposition voters into a few districts to reduce their influence elsewhere, while cracking spreads them thinly across many districts, diluting their voting power. Both are tools of an arsenal designed to rig the outcome of elections in favor of those in control of the redistricting process.

Current technology has escalated the precision with which parties can gerrymander. Data analytics allow political operatives to predict voting patterns at an almost granular level, evolving gerrymandering from an art form into a science—where every line drawn is a calculated move in a larger power game.

The Supreme Court has grappled with the legality of gerrymandering. In instances like *Shaw v. Reno* and more recently in *Rucho v. Common Cause*, the Court's decisions reflected a reluctance to intervene in what are seen as political questions. Nonetheless, dissenting justices have noted the threat gerrymandering poses to democratic principles.

Responses to this manipulation have varied, highlighting a divide in strategy. Some states have introduced independent redistricting commissions intending to depoliticize the process. However, while these commissions aim to create fairer districts, questions remain regarding their efficacy and the potential for residual partisan influence.

Moreover, gerrymandering has significant ramifications beyond electoral outcomes. It affects the responsiveness of elected officials to their constituents. When a district is safely in the hands of one party, the incentive to cater to the broader needs of the district's voters diminishes. This often results in more polarized politicians who cater to the extremes of their party base rather than the electorate at large.

There are also implications for public policy. Gerrymandering can lead to skewed representation that does not accurately reflect the demographics of the population. Consequently, policy decisions may favor the interests of a limited group rather than addressing the concerns of the entire community. This exacerbates social fragmentation, further deepening divides between different societal groups.

The concept of 'one person, one vote' is fundamentally undermined by gerrymandering. It enables a minority of voters to exert disproportionate control over the political landscape, which is antithetical to democratic ideals. The rising awareness of this has led to widespread demands for reform and the establishment of a more equitable districting process.

Social movements and grassroots campaigns have begun to shift the discourse around gerrymandering. Citizens are becoming increasingly educated on the issue and are beginning to hold their representatives accountable for unfair districting practices. As an expression of direct democracy, these activities showcase the potential for collective action to achieve change within the system.

Legal scholars and political theorists debate the best methods to curtail gerrymandering, with some advocating for computer-generated, non-partisan maps, others pushing for proportional representation, or suggesting increased federal oversight in the redistricting process. These debates signal a crucial public engagement with the mechanisms of democracy and a shared pursuit of more equitable representation.

Understanding gerrymandering and districting is fundamental to analyzing America's political landscape. These practices speak volumes about how control is consolidated and maintained, and they provide insight into the wider dynamics of power and division. As America grapples with gerrymandering's implications and seeks remedies, the continued monitoring of districting practices remains a critical avenue in the fight for a more just and representative democracy.

As we explore the larger American conquest strategy, it is clear that gerrymandering serves as a powerful tool in shaping political outcomes and public policy. The influence of gerrymandering on the nation's ideological divides cannot be overstated, nor can the need for solutions that ensure fair and democratic representation for all American citizens.

Chapter 4:
Economic Divides

In the previous chapter, we untangled the intricacies of political ruptures that have shaped the American landscape. Let's shift our lens to a perhaps even more tangible aspect of division: Economics. The chasm between the affluent and the impoverished has never been more pronounced, its edges hardened by policies that often favor wealth accumulation at the top tiers. As we dissect the anatomy of this vast economic divide, we'll explore how the expansion of wealth for a select few has led to stifled opportunities for the many, affecting not only individual prospects but also the collective economic dynamism. It isn't just about who has more; instead, it's a reflection of an underlying system that determines who gets to accumulate wealth and who doesn't even get a seat at the table. The palpable tension between economic classes has grown more charged, raising urgent questions about the sustainability of a system that seems to perpetuate, if not widen, these divides. Subsequent sections will delve into the specificities of wealth gaps and policies, but it's imperative to recognize that the economic stratification we witness is a result of deliberate choices made within corridors of power. Choices that can be redirected, should the political will be mustered for the sake of an equitable future.

The Wealth Gap

Within the fabric of American society, the wealth gap stands as a stark testament to the persistent economic divides that have, in many respects, defined the nation. As we turn our lens to this pressing issue, one can't overlook the profound implications of such disparity: it's not just a chasm separating the affluent from the less fortunate—it's a canyon that has been carved out by years of strategic conquest, both economic and political. The figures are more than sobering; they're a clarion call for introspection and action. While average incomes may appear to rise, the quintessence of true wealth—comprising real estate, investments, and inheritances—continues to concentrate in the hands of a few, fueling a cycle of privilege and power that cascades across generations. This concentration of wealth not only undermines the ethos of equal opportunity but also reinforces social stratifications and lays the groundwork for policies that exacerbate polarization, which will be delved into further in subsequent chapters. Hence, to grasp the roots of today's division, one must confront the realities of the wealth gap—a divide that silently tightens its grip on the American dream, shaping lives and futures in its unrelenting hold.

Policies and Polarization The United States, while often celebrated for its diversity and democratic ideals, is also a tapestry of divided entities, drawn not just along the lines of wealth but also political affiliation. As we explore the nuances of economic disparities, it becomes increasingly clear that the policies enacted by governing bodies do not merely address these differences but, in many instances, exacerbate them. This section scrutinizes the intricate ways in which legislative decisions have contributed to the fissures within American society.

The wealth gap, an already prominent issue in American fiscal landscapes, is directly influenced by the policies that encourage or indeed hinder wealth accumulation and distribution. Tax codes, social welfare programs, and labor laws are some of the most tangible examples where policy can either bridge the economic divide or widen it. For instance, tax cuts that disproportionately benefit the wealthiest individuals can lead to an increase in income inequality, deepening the chasm between socio-economic classes.

Poignantly, the allocation of funding for public services, such as education and healthcare, is another area where policies play an essential role in either leveling the playing field or tilting it. When funding for schools is tied to property taxes, a cyclical polarization is manifest; affluent areas receive more substantial resources for education, thus facilitating better outcomes for the residents of those areas and perpetuating a cycle of privilege.

Moving beyond the fiscal realm, the political landscape is indeed shaped and reshaped by legislation that affects voting access and representation. Policies that introduce strict voter ID laws, limit early voting, or purge voter rolls can suppress the political voice of certain demographics, particularly those from lower socio-economic groups. These actions add another layer to the polarizing effects of economic policies, as those who are disenfranchised economically are often the same individuals facing disenfranchisement at the polls.

The influence of lobbyists and special interest groups in crafting legislation cannot be understated within this context. These entities, which often represent the interests of the wealthy and powerful, exert considerable influence over elected officials. The resulting policies may cater to the preferences of the elite, thus perpetuating their economic dominance and ensuring the persistence of polarization.

Furthermore, the political rhetoric employed by candidates and elected officials plays a significant role in deepening ideological divides. When leaders use divisive language to garner support, they create a tribal atmosphere in politics, one that construes policy debates as zero-sum battles between "us" and "them." This framing transforms every political discourse into an opportunity for further polarization, reducing complex issues to overly simplistic dichotomies.

It's also essential to discuss the influence that social policies have on economic polarization. For instance, debates surrounding minimum wage laws reflect differing ideologies about the role of government in the market. Those opposing an increase in the minimum wage argue that it would lead to job losses and stifle economic growth, while proponents believe it's a necessary step towards reducing income inequality and providing a living wage for the lowest earners. These differing perspectives result in policy stalemates that entrench existing economic disparities.

One cannot overlook the profound impact of healthcare policy in the conversation about economic polarization. The United States' unique system, which often ties healthcare to employment, creates a divide between those who can afford quality healthcare and those who cannot. Legislation aiming to reform healthcare, such as the Affordable Care Act, has become fiercely contentious, illustrating the profound ideological battle over government's role in providing social benefits.

The interstate implications of policies also contribute to polarization. State governments play a significant role in shaping economic landscapes through their own tax and regulatory policies. This has led to a situation where states are often pitted against each other in a race to attract businesses, using tax incentives and deregulation as their main tools. These practices can have the side effect of deepening disparities both within and between states.

To consider the effects of globalization within this framework is also vital. Trade policies affect domestic industries in different ways; tariffs, trade agreements, and regulations have the power to make or break entire economic sectors. The polarizing impact of these policies becomes evident when considering whose interests are protected and whose are left vulnerable in the global marketplace.

The dichotomy between rural and urban economic opportunities is another facet of the policy-induced polarization. Rural areas in the United States often do not receive the same level of investment or economic diversification as urban centers, creating an inherent economic disparity. Policies that fail to address the unique needs of these communities contribute to a sense of abandonment and resentment, fueling political polarization as residents turn to candidates who promise to redress these perceived imbalances.

Education policy is a particularly poignant example of how long-term polarization takes root. Funding disparities lead to divergent educational outcomes, which in turn affect employment opportunities and earning potential. Education, ideally a means of upward mobility, can become a deeply divisive issue as policies falter in providing equitable opportunities for all.

The intersection of criminal justice and economic policy also cannot be overlooked. The war on drugs, mandatory minimum sentencing, and cash bail systems disproportionately affect minorities and the poor. These policies not only exacerbate existing economic disparities but also serve to entrench them systemically through the criminalization of poverty.

Lastly, the transformative potential of technology has a polarizing counterpart in policy. As automation and digital transitions reshape the job market, there is a critical need for policies that facilitate workforce adaptation and retraining. Without such measures, the technological divide could manifest as yet another axis of economic polarization, leaving behind those who are unable to navigate the changing landscape of work.

In summary, while economic policies are often posited as vehicles for prosperity and fairness, their formulation and implementation can, paradoxically, foster polarization. This reality underscores the necessity of a nuanced and holistic approach to policy-making, one that acknowledges and addresses the complex interplay between economic prosperity and societal unity. As we delve further into how social fragmentation compounds these effects, it becomes increasingly clear that the issue of polarization is multifaceted, with roots that extend deeply into the fabric of American policies and politics.

Chapter 5:
Social Fragmentation

Moving beyond the economic stratification discussed in Chapter 4, we now examine another profound contributor to the social landscape: the disquieting aspect of social fragmentation. The American conquest strategy has contributed significantly to societal divisions, not just in terms of wealth, but also in the intricate fabrics of cultural, racial, and ethnic identities. It is here that the mosaic of American society displays its fault lines most glaringly. Through political rhetoric, policy-making, and the instrumentalization of cultural differences, groups have been systematically positioned against one another, calcifying into blocks that struggle to engage in a genuinely national discourse. This chasm extends beyond mere disagreement, morphing into a deep-seated schism that threatens the very idea of a united collective. The tendrils of this division reach into the daily lives of citizens, affecting everything from neighborhood compositions to educational opportunities, mirroring a historical pattern of deliberate disunion. As we delve into this chapter, we'll uncover the underlying currents that perpetuate segregation and explore how such fractures not only undermine social cohesion but also serve the overarching strategies of control and conquest that have shaped the nation.

Race and Ethnicity

In the mosaic that composes the United States, race and ethnicity have frequently been used as a chisel, cleaving society along distinct lines.

26

Within the grand strategy of American conquest, these identifiers have transcended mere descriptors, transforming into potent levers for social control and political maneuvering. Racial and ethnic distinctions, enforced both by law and cultural norms, have engendered an environment where unity is persistently undermined by the whispers of division. Legacy policies have calcified into systemic barriers that, even now, dictate socioeconomic strata and access to opportunity. Far from disappearing into the melting pot, these divisions have been exacerbated, serving as a stark reminder of the pervasiveness of segregation in both physical communities and the national psyche. As a fragment of the broader discussion within "Social Fragmentation," understanding how race and ethnicity inform American disunity is crucial; it uncovers how the amalgamation of diverse peoples can be strategically distorted to maintain a status quo ripe for exploitation.

The Immigration Debate The discussion on immigration is often at the forefront of America's road to prosperity and conflict. From a historical perspective, the nation founded on the principle of being a melting pot now faces an increasingly complex array of opinions surrounding its immigration policies. This debate ensnares politicians, citizens, and immigrants alike in a web of ideological clashes, economic apprehensions, and cultural negotiations.

Immigration remains one of the most contested issues within the broader landscape of American conquest strategy. To understand the depths of this controversy, it's imperative to examine the philosophical roots that shape perspectives on immigration. There's a palpable tension between those advocating for the nation to uphold its legacy as a land of opportunity, and those who perceive immigration as a threat to national security, economic stability, or cultural identity.

Key to the debate is the economic aspect of immigration. Proponents assert that immigrants fill critical labor gaps, contribute to innovation, and stimulate economic growth. Conversely, opponents argue that unchecked immigration may suppress wages, burden welfare systems, and lead to job scarcity for native-born citizens. The data on these issues is invariably complex, allowing for selective interpretation that fuels the partisan divide.

The conversation also entails a significant cultural component. Questions about assimilation, cultural retention, and the shaping of American identity form the crux of many discussions. For some, the influx of different cultures enriches the American tapestry. For others, there are fears about the dilution of traditional values and the potential for cultural clashes that could disrupt societal harmony.

National security concerns occupy a substantial portion of the immigration discourse; the emphasis here is often on border control. The narrative intertwines with xenophobic strands, perpetuating stereotypes and, at times, resulting in discriminatory policies. The push for stronger border measures contends with humanitarian appeals to treat migrants and refugees with dignity and within international legal frameworks.

On the legal front, the differentiation between legal and illegal immigration serves as a significant flashpoint. Legal immigrants who navigate the bureaucratic labyrinth to enter the U.S. legally are often juxtaposed against undocumented immigrants who, due to economic hardship or fleeing persecution, circumvent the legal routes. The path to citizenship or legalization for the latter group is a matter of heated debate, impacting millions of lives and families.

The political chessboard sees both major parties leveraging the immigration debate to mobilize their base. For some politicians, adopting a hardline stance against immigration spells a rallying cry that consolidates support. Others, by championing more inclusive policies, seek to capture the growing demographic of naturalized citizens and their allies. This dichotomy is clear-cut in platforms and policy proposals during election cycles.

The repercussions of the immigration debate are not confined within the boundaries of the U.S. As global migration trends intensify due to conflict, climate change, and economic disparities, America's immigration policies fundamentally influence and reflect its international relations and strategic positioning.

The social fabric of communities across the U.S. reflects the ongoing immigration debate. Cities that have traditionally been gateways for immigrants often witness more progressive attitudes and policies. In contrast, communities unaccustomed to immigration may display resistance, reinforcing nationalistic sentiments that can erupt into local tensions or propel restrictive state legislations.

Demographic shifts resulting from immigration patterns present profound long-term implications for political representation. As communities evolve, so do their needs and the political landscape. The diversity heralded by new immigrant populations challenges existing power structures, instigating a reevaluation of policies and representation at local and national levels.

The interplay of education and immigration is a critical aspect often overshadowed in the debate. The pursuit of human capital via international students and skilled immigrants is integral to maintaining technological and scientific leadership. Yet, this aspect must be balanced against the concerns of educational access for native-born citizens, where competition for limited resources can create friction.

Reform discussions ebb and flow with the currents of public opinion and political will. Comprehensive immigration reform has long been the elusive goal for successive administrations, hinting at the deep-seated complexity and contention of the issue. Each proposal is dissected and debated with ferocity, reflecting the importance placed on the future of immigration policy.

The role of activism cannot be understated in the immigration debate. Advocacy groups for and against various immigration policies are instrumental in shaping the narrative and spurring action among legislators and communities. These organizations wield significant influence, aligning with broader ideological movements and contributing to the polarization of views.

Through it all, the human element is omnipresent. Behind the politics, policies, and polemics are real people whose lives are directly affected by the outcomes of this debate. Families seeking better futures, workers aspiring for fair conditions, and individuals fleeing turmoil – their stories add emotional depth to the discussion, reminding society of the personal stakes at hand.

Ultimately, the immigration debate is a microcosm of the larger dynamics at play in the American conquest strategy – a strategy that, by necessity, grapples with the question of how to reconcile the nation's founding ideals with the realities of a changing world. The way forward hinges on America's ability to navigate this debate with a balance of pragmatism, compassion, and strategic vision, ensuring its legacy as a land of opportunity without compromising its societal integrity.

Chapter 6:
Global Echoes

The influence of the American conquest strategy extends far beyond its borders, resonating across continents in a variety of nuanced ways. In "Global Echoes," we delve into the profound impact that U.S. military and political maneuvers have had on the global stage. By exporting its approach to leverage power dynamics, the United States has often catalyzed strategic affiliations and shadowy coalitions that adjust the balance of governance in myriad regimes. Not only does the echo of American strategy resound in international corridors of power, but it also reverberates through societies struggling with democracy, leaving behind a complex legacy of political discourse and interventionism. While American tactics abroad may carry a promise of stability, they also run the risk of perpetuating existing divisions or even creating new ones—often with unintended consequences that last decades. This chapter posits that to truly comprehend the breadth of American influence and the transnational nature of strategic division, one must thoroughly examine both the overt and covert actions taken in the name of American interests and how these give shape to our contemporary world order.

American Tactics Abroad

In evaluating the United States' international strategy, it is critical to examine the various tactics employed to project power beyond its borders. These approaches often capitalize on the existing social and political fractures within nations, leveraging them to advance American interests. At the forefront are nuanced forms of intervention—from fostering opposition movements to the discrete backing of sympathetic leaders—which can set the stage for future influence and control. These operations are not merely a relic of the Cold War; they've evolved with technology, embracing cyber-operations and information warfare to sway elections and gather intelligence. Beneath the surface of public discourse, these measures have intricate long-term effects on the global stage, including the perpetuation of conflict, the manipulation of emerging economies, and the shaping of international norms. As such, understanding the mechanics of these maneuvers is indispensable for grasping the global impact of U.S. policy and its reverberations in geopolitical arenas worldwide.

Influencing Foreign Divisions In analyzing the American conquest strategy and its expansive reach, one cannot overlook the deft maneuvers it has executed upon foreign divisions. The United States, both historically and in modern times, has evolved its approach to influence the international political chessboard by leveraging divisions within foreign countries to promote its national interests.

First and foremost, it is essential to recognize how the U.S. has established its soft power—the ability to shape the preferences and attitudes of others through attraction rather than coercion. This is achieved by projecting its cultural dominance, political values, and economic promises. The spread of American culture through movies, music, and brands carries with it a broader ideological influence that can predispose foreign populations to a more favorable view of U.S. policies and initiatives.

An intricate part of American strategy includes the nurturing of economic relationships tailored to open up or exploit rifts within emerging markets or politically shaky regions. Trade deals and foreign aid are two-edged swords; while providing necessary development or rescue, they also create dependence, thereby giving the U.S. significant leverage over domestic policies within those nations.

Diplomacy is another tool oft-employed in the art of influencing foreign divisions. U.S. foreign policy has, at times, been to support specific political or social factions within countries—those that align more closely with American interests. This tends to insert the U.S. into ongoing conflicts or exacerbate existing tensions, with the aim of shaping the outcome to favor American geopolitical goals.

Intelligence operations, meanwhile, are the more covert arm of American influence. Through intelligence gathering and surveillance, the U.S. gains insight into the vulnerabilities of other nations. The strategic release or withholding of such information can tip scales in internal political landscapes, incite unrest, or sway foreign elections.

Military interventions, whether direct or through proxy actors, have a historical significance in shaping foreign governments and their internal divisions. Decisions to support coups, fund rebel groups, or deploy military force have indelibly altered the trajectories of countries around the world, often leaving a legacy of division and instability in exchange for short-term strategic gains.

Marketing democracy has been among the nobler fronts for influencing foreign divisions, by advocating for free and fair elections, rule of law, and human rights. However, these endeavors often disguise ulterior objectives and thrust nascent democracies into a turbulent process of political maturation with the side effect of widened societal fault lines.

When it comes to extending its international law enforcement, the U.S. has frequently collaborated with foreign governments to dismantle transnational criminal organizations. Despite the obvious benefits of such actions, this intersection of law enforcement and international policy can lead to a disturbing imbalance within local governance structures if not managed with a balanced hand.

Information technology and the digital space have evolved into an arena of surreptitious influence operations. U.S. involvement in cyber initiatives has been both defensive and offensive, aiming to protect its interests and weaken adversarial alliances. Social media manipulation, for example, has been used to foment dissent or project favorable narratives within foreign civil societies.

U.S. educational and cultural exchange programs are less abrasive methods for exerting influence. Through such avenues, foreign nationals exposed to American values and practices may return to their homelands as inadvertent vectors for U.S.-aligned ideologies, possibly contributing to divisions back home as their new perspectives clash with local traditions.

Crisis exploitation, unfortunately, is a recurring theme in the annals of international influence. The U.S. has not shied away from using economic or humanitarian crises to push for reforms or changes in leadership that cater to its strategic vistas, often highlighting divisions to justify interventionist policies.

Trade policies have been a distinct aspect of this influence through preferential treatment extended to certain industries or sanctions imposed on others. The resultant economic pressure can often lead to a redistribution of power within the affected countries, aggravating class divisions and regional disparities.

At diplomatic forums such as the United Nations, the U.S. has played a principal role in directing discourses that define international norms and interventions. These platforms are used to consolidate alliances and outline the narrative of global conflicts, placing pressure on countries to choose sides along lines forged by U.S. diplomacy.

Lastly, humanitarian aid, while saving countless lives and contributing to the development of low-income countries, may also bolster or undermine particular groups within those countries. The conditionality of such aid and its allocation can lead to perceived or actual imbalances and perpetuate divisions at the local or national level.

Effective as they are, these diverse strategies for influencing foreign divisions come with an array of ethical conundrums and long-term repercussions. The interplay between foreign policy objectives and the real impact on global communities must be acknowledged as the U.S. navigates its role on the world stage, wielding its considerable ability to shape not only the destinies of nations but the cohesion of their societies.

Chapter 7:
The Future of Unity

As we pivot from the disquieting ripple effects of America's conquest strategy on global arenas to prospects closer to heart, we encounter a pressing challenge: the mending of a fragmented nation. The discourse surrounding unity is replete with a myriad of layers and complexities, yet it is an attainable horizon that demands our unwavering commitment. If history is a guidepost for what's to come, the wisdom gleaned from past attempts to bridge divides can chart our course forward. It is incumbent upon us to scrutinize our shared identity and harness the collective will to overcome partisan chasms. By fostering dialogue that elevates understanding over rhetoric and leveraging policies that are rooted in equity, there exists potential for a renaissance of American consensus. The fabric of the nation, weathered by the storms of dissent, may find reparation in a unity that does not entail uniformity but thrives on the rich tapestry of its diversity. The future of unity, thus, rests not only in the dismantling of systemic divisions but in the architecture of a society where the very notion of a conquest strategy becomes an archaism, replaced by strategies for inclusive growth and a renewed covenant of citizenship.

Overcoming Division

In addressing the formidable task of bridging the chasms carved by division, we must first recognize that unity is not the quelling of diversity but the harmonious synchronization of its many facets.

Mending the ruptures in the fabric of our society can't be a passive wish but an active pursuit requiring engagement and dialogue. It is through the rigorous examination of our shared values and the collective acknowledgment of mutual aspirations that a more cohesive future may be forged. Encouraging empathetic discourse and nurturing a culture that values compromise over conquest are not mere niceties but necessities for a thriving republic. Bonds reinforced by understanding and mutual respect, rather than dominance, pave the way towards a semblance of accord. Our strategies to heal must be as meticulously executed as those that have been used to segment, ensuring we broker an era where unity acts as the cornerstone of our national ethos, rather than an elusive ideal.

Pathways to Reconciliation Understanding the complexity and depth of the American conquest strategy leads us to a crucial juncture where contemplation changes into action. History has furnished us ample evidence of how division can be sown and festers within the fabric of a society. Now, it is time to deliberate on the avenues that can heal the rifts and bring about reconciliation among communities fragmented by chronic contention.

Reconciliation is a process – a nuanced and layered journey towards mutual understanding and respect. It starts with acknowledging the past, understanding the intricate dynamics of the present, and forging a vision for the future that includes all facets of society. This is not merely about finding a middle ground; it is about reconstructing a shared space, where competing narratives can coexist with dignity and equality.

One of the primary steps toward reconciliation is the promotion of historical accuracy and truth-telling. Societies can only move forward when they are willing to examine their past without bias. It can be an uncomfortable process, but it lays the foundations for genuine dialogue. In the context of the American conquest strategy, this means revisiting and recognizing the strategies and policies that have contributed to division and acknowledging the suffering they have caused.

Another pathway is the active encouragement of inclusive politics. The political ruptures outlined in earlier chapters can be addressed by reforms that ensure fair representation and engagement for all segments of society. Election systems require overhauls to eliminate practices like gerrymandering and to minimize polarization. Additionally, the importance of transparency cannot be overstated – it fosters trust in the system and its leaders.

A focus on education as a tool for reconciliation is also paramount. An educational curriculum that embraces a broad narrative can significantly alter perceptions and attitudes. Through education, individuals can be taught to be analytical and empathetic, recognizing propaganda and ideological wedges for what they are. Education encourages individuals to step out of their echo chambers and engage with diverse perspectives.

Economic divides further exacerbate societal tensions, as outlined earlier. Therefore, policies aimed at bridging the wealth gap, such as progressive taxation, improved social safety nets, and equal access to opportunities, will serve as integral pathways to reconciliation. Economic empowerment and stability often lead to a more harmonious society, reducing the 'us versus them' mentality.

Addressing social fragmentation requires a comprehensive strategy that discourages discrimination based on race, ethnicity, or immigration status. It necessitates the implementation of laws and social initiatives that promote equality and counteract systemic bias. These efforts must also be supplemented by societal movements that encourage introspection and collective responsibility in combating ingrained prejudices.

Furthermore, in a world that is interconnected as never before, the American conquest strategy's influence on international relations needs to be reevaluated. The promotion of peace over divisiveness abroad can have a significant and positive ripple effect domestically, reinforcing the commitment to unity and shared goals.

Just as much as there is a need for systemic reform, there is a necessity for grassroots initiatives that encourage community building and collaboration. Local organizations, civic groups, and neighborhood associations can foster environments for face-to-face interactions, helping to humanize opposing viewpoints and establish common ground.

Dialogue and restorative justice processes have proven to be effective in soothing historical wounds and present-day misunderstandings. Structured forums where people can talk openly about their experiences and grievances can lead to empathy and collective healing. These should not only be accessible but keenly promoted in communities, enterprises, and institutions alike.

It is equally important to have symbolic acts of reconciliation. These can sometimes be dismissed as merely token gestures, yet they have the power to resonate deeply with the public's consciousness. Monuments, holidays, and memorials that pay homage to victims of divisive strategies can help acknowledge and remember the lessons of the past.

Indeed, the media holds a significant key to reconciliation. Responsible journalism must rise above the fray of sensationalism and commit to unbiased and informative reporting. The media has a duty to help steer the public discourse towards constructive conversations, debunk misinformation, and promote narratives that unite rather than divide.

Technology, too, plays a role in the pursuit of unity. Social media platforms and online communities have the potential to be harnessed as spaces for building bridges rather than walls. The digital landscape should amplify voices of reconciliation and be engineered to discourage the dissemination of harmful and divisive content.

To realize these pathways to reconciliation, leadership at every level must be held accountable. Leaders must exemplify the principles of unity, carrying out their duties with integrity, compassion, and a steadfast commitment to the public good. They need to engage with all factions and be seen as representing the entirety of their constituencies, not just those who support them.

Ultimately, the journey to reconciliation is continuous and sprawling, involving each individual's responsibility towards creating a more equitable and unified society. Every step taken, no matter how small, accumulates to impact the collective trajectory towards a healed nation. Parse through the American conquest strategy and its legacies, and one can discern the framework for a more cohesive future, should we choose to take the path to reconciliation.

As this section draws to a close, it becomes evident that the avenues for reconciliation are many, each requiring commitment, empathy, and a vision for a more inclusive community. This is not an exhaustive list, but it provides the scaffolding upon which society can build and strengthen its bonds, steering away from the divisive tactics of the past towards the promise of a unified future.

Conclusion

As we have navigated the complexities of American conquest strategy throughout this book, we have uncovered the multilayered and intricate processes that have shaped not only the United States as we see it today, but also its global interactions. We've traced its roots back to historical precursors, delved deeply into the role of ideology, surveyed political, economic, and social fractures, and considered America's influence on the world stage.

The in-depth exploration of these facets offers us a sobering portrait of a nation grappling with the consequences of its own strategies for dominion and control. The repercussions of these strategies are far-reaching, contributing to the current climate of division that poses significant challenges to the fabric of American society. As we reflect on this landscape, it's evident that understanding these dynamics is not merely an academic exercise; it has tangible implications for the lives of individuals and communities.

Despite these challenges, we've also uncovered the seeds of resiliency and the potential for transformation. Our discussion has pointed the way toward pathways for reconciliation and unity, suggesting that even amid division, there is hope for a more cohesive and inclusive future.

The conquest strategy, with its focus on gain and superiority, has left indelible marks on the political and electoral machinery of the nation. Gerrymandering and districting show with clarity the extent to which the drive for control has perverted the democratic ideals on which the country was founded. Yet while these tactics have historically served to entrench power, they have also ignited calls for reform and increased awareness around electoral integrity.

The economic divides that we see are a testament to the entrenched nature of the conquest mindset. The widening wealth gap is not merely a statistic but a narrative of disparities and a series of barriers to equal opportunity. It is a story of policies and polarization that have benefited a few while leaving many behind. This economic narrative has been deeply intertwined with social divisions, especially those of race and ethnicity, further exacerbating the notion of 'us versus them' within our borders.

When we consider social fragmentation, it's crucial to recognize that discussions around race and the immigration debate are reflective of how conquest strategies have come home to roost. Such issues, while seemingly domestic, are deeply informed by the historical American interventionist playbook. The division sown at home mirrors the divisive tactics often used abroad—a fact that underscores the interconnectivity of domestic and international policies.

The echoes of America's internal strategies resonate in its foreign affairs, shaping other nations in ways that often lead to a mirroring of the divides seen within its own soil. As we've seen, the tactical spread of influence and the fostering of foreign schisms is not without repercussions, and the global community is very much attuned to the implications of American strategies for division or unity.

In confronting the pressing questions around how such divisions can be healed, it's clear that intentional, persistent effort and a commitment to dialogue and understanding will be essential. The pathways to reconciliation demand both a reckoning with the past and a progressive, forward-thinking approach. The pursuit of unity is not an endgame but a continual process of engagement and learning.

Therefore, as we close the final chapter on the analysis of American conquest strategy, we're called to not only reflect on the past and present but also to actively shape our future. We must leverage our understanding of the fractures to rebuild stronger, more inclusive structures in their stead. This book has been a journey—a deep dive into the reasons behind the divides and an opening of doors to conversations that could bridge the gaps.

American society, while facing division, is not without its strengths. Its diversity, democratic ideals, and legacy of innovation provide a foundation upon which unity can be fostered. Moreover, the active engagement of its citizenry in the process of nation-building offers a beacon of hope—the pursuit of a more perfect union is an intrinsic part of the American identity.

This analysis, ultimately, is not a call to despair but an invitation to action. It asks of its readers to be informed, to question, and to engage with the historical and current dynamics that have shaped and continue to shape this nation. It is a call to become part of the very fabric of change—to be the thinkers, communicators, and leaders who can forge paths toward a less divided future.

What unfolds from here on out is not set in stone. The course of history has always been shaped by the actions, large and small, of individuals and groups who strive for something better. Our knowledge of the past and present empowers us to make informed choices for the future. It equips us with the tools to discern truth from propaganda, to recognize the artificiality of divisions formed for conquest, and to embrace the common humanity that can unite us.

Let this conclusive reflection serve as both an end and a beginning—an end to the analysis within these pages, and the beginning of a personal and collective journey toward understanding, unity, and a reshaping of the American conquest strategy into a narrative of collaboration and mutual respect. The task ahead is formidable, but it is within such challenges that the true spirit of a people emerges. The future awaits, and it is ours to define.